POPE LEO XIV

Making a Difference as the First American Pope

By Therese M. Shea

People Who Make a Difference

KidHaven PUBLISHING

Published in 2026 by
KidHaven Publishing, an Imprint of Greenhaven Publishing, LLC
2544 Clinton St.
Buffalo, NY 14224

Designer: Deanna Lepovich
Editor: Katie Kawa

Photo credits: Cover, pp. 5 (main), 13, 20 Marco Iacobucci Epp/Shutterstock.com; p. 5 (inset) Peter Hermes Furian/Shutterstock.com; p. 7 Pope Leo XIV childhood home/Wikimedia Commons; pp. 8, 11 (main) Photos courtesy of the Midwest Augustinian Province of Our Mother of Good Counsel; p. 9 Dorr E. Felt/Wikimedia Commons; p. 11 (inset) iryna shorokhova/Shutterstock.com; p. 15 Santa María Catedral - Chiclayo/Wikimedia Commons; p. 17 Riccardo De Luca - Update/Shutterstock.com; p. 18 Erin Alexis Randolph/Shutterstock.com; p. 21 T.Sumaetho/Shutterstock.com.

Cataloging-in-Publication Data

Names: Shea, Therese, author.
Title: Pope Leo XIV: making a difference as the first American pope / Therese M. Shea
Description: Buffalo, NY : KidHaven Publishing, 2026. | Series: People who make a difference | Includes glossary and index.
Identifiers: ISBN 9781534552333 (pbk.) | ISBN 9781534552340 (library bound) | ISBN 9781534552357 (ebook)
Subjects: LCSH: Leo XIV, Pope, 1955–Juvenile literature. | Popes–Biography–Juvenile literature.
Classification: LCC BX1378.7 S543 2026 | DDC 282.092–dc23

Printed in the United States of America

CONTENTS

"WE HAVE A POPE!"

On May 8, 2025, in the tiny European country of Vatican City, white smoke rose from a **chimney**. Millions around the world had been watching that chimney. They cheered. They knew what the smoke meant.

A **cardinal** announced, "Habemus papam!" This is Latin for "We have a pope!" A new pope, the leader of the Roman Catholic Church, had been elected. His name was Robert Prevost. He was the first pope born in the United States. Robert chose a new name as pope: Leo XIV (14). He was ready to use his new role, or job, to make a difference.

In His Words

"Greetings to Rome and to the world! Peace be with all of you!"

— First speech as pope as reported by *Vatican News* from May 8, 2025

Pope Leo XIV lives in Vatican City. This country is surrounded by Rome, which is Italy's capital city.

THE POPE'S CHILDHOOD

Robert Francis Prevost was born on September 14, 1955, in Chicago, Illinois. His father, Louis, was a school principal, and his mother, Mildred, was a librarian. Robert, who was called Rob by his family, was the youngest of three boys.

Robert's older brothers have said Robert wanted to be a **priest** from a young age. Even as a child, he liked to "play priest." He also liked racing toy cars with friends and playing street hockey with the rest of the neighborhood kids.

In His Words

"I was born in the United States ... But my grandparents were all **immigrants**, French, Spanish ..."

— Interview with RAI Italian public television from May 2025

This was Pope Leo's childhood home
in Dolton, Illinois, south of Chicago.

PREPARING FOR THE PRIESTHOOD

In 1969, Robert began attending St. Augustine Seminary High School in Michigan. It was for boys who were considering becoming priests. He went on to Villanova University near Philadelphia, Pennsylvania, and received a **degree** in math in 1977.

Robert then studied to be a priest in both Chicago and Rome, Italy. He was **ordained** in 1982. He joined the Order of Saint Augustine. These priests, called Augustinians, promise to be poor and share what they have with their community. They promise to help others in need and spread their faith.

In His Words

"As an Augustinian, having a rich community built on the ability to share with others what happens to us, to be open to others, has been one of the greatest gifts I have been given in this life."

— Interview on the Order of St. Augustine website from September 30, 2023

Part of St. Augustine Seminary is shown here. Robert lived there as a teen, only going home for summers and holidays. His school friends remember that "Bob" was smart and quiet, but had a good sense of humor.

LIFE IN PERU

In 1985, Father Robert (as he was called then) was sent to the Augustinian **mission** in Chulucanas, Peru. Many people were poor there. He traveled around to mud-brick churches on horseback and on foot. He organized, or planned, activities for the children there. He hired coaches to teach sports to keep young people away from crime.

In the 1980s, the Peruvian government and **guerrilla** forces were fighting in the area. The priests in Chulucanas were told to leave or be killed. A bomb exploded in one of their churches! Father Robert—called Padre Roberto by the Peruvians—chose to stay and help.

In His Words

"If you love God, then you also need to be showing that by loving your neighbor and that the two go hand in hand."

— Interview with the Catholic News Service from October 29, 2012

This is a photo of Father Robert Prevost as a young priest, meeting Pope John Paul II, who was pope from 1978 to 2005. Also shown here is a map of Peru with important locations from Pope Leo's life labeled.

FROM TRUJILLO TO WORLD TRAVELER

In 1988, Father Robert joined the mission in Trujillo, Peru. He had several responsibilities, or duties, there over 11 years. He was head of a seminary. He taught church laws. He worked with the poor. Many Peruvians had lost their homes because of the guerrilla fighting and were poor.

In 1999, Father Robert accepted a leadership role in the Order of St. Augustine in Chicago. He had to leave Peru. In 2001, he was elected the head of the whole order. He lived in Rome and traveled the world for several years.

In His Words

"I also really enjoy ... traveling—seeing and enjoying new and **diverse** places."

— Interview on the Order of St. Augustine website from September 30, 2023

Peruvians and Pope Leo have a special connection. When he left Trujillo, a party was held to honor him. The mayor said, "Trujillo is a better place because of Father Bob's having been here." Here, Peruvians display a banner in May 2025 showing the new pope they are there to support him.

BISHOP PREVOST

Father Robert returned to Peru in 2014. The next year, Pope Francis, who was the pope at the time, named him **Bishop** of Chiclayo, a city and **diocese** in northwest Peru. Robert Prevost became a Peruvian citizen in 2015 too.

In 2017, hundreds of thousands of **refugees** fled fighting and poverty in Venezuela and sought safety in Peru. Bishop Prevost welcomed them to Chiclayo and helped find housing and food for them. In 2022 and 2023, Chiclayo had terrible floods. The bishop helped deliver food to those who needed it. He carried heavy rice sacks on his back into the mountains.

In His Words

"A greeting to all and especially to my beloved diocese of Chiclayo, in Peru."

— First speech as pope as reported by *Vatican News* from May 8, 2025

This is St. Mary's Cathedral in Chiclayo, Peru, where Robert Prevost was bishop from 2015 to 2023. He was part of the community and listened to people's ideas.

CARDINAL PREVOST

In January 2023, Pope Francis asked Bishop Prevost to come to Vatican City. The pope wanted him to take a new job, helping to choose new bishops as well as oversee the Catholic Church in Central and South America. Robert accepted, though he was sad to leave Peru. Pope Francis made Robert Prevost a cardinal in September 2023.

Pope Francis died on April 21, 2025. All the cardinals from around the world came together in Vatican City to elect a new pope. Cardinal Prevost was one of them.

In His Words

"You [Pope Francis] know that I am very happy in Peru ... but if you ask me to take on a new role in the church, I will accept."

— Interview on the Order of St. Augustine website from September 30, 2023

Pope Francis places a red biretta, a special hat, on Robert Prevost, making him a cardinal.

INTO THE CONCLAVE

The gathering of the cardinals to select a pope is called a papal conclave. It takes place in secret. The cardinals aren't allowed to talk to anyone but each other. They pray and talk together. They vote for a new leader without opinions from the outside world.

In the 2025 conclave, 89 votes were needed out of a total of 133 for someone to become pope. Sometimes it takes many days to elect a pope. However, Cardinal Prevost got the votes needed on the second day of the conclave.

In His Words

"I'm an American — I can't be elected."

— Text from then-Cardinal Prevost to a friend before the 2025 conclave

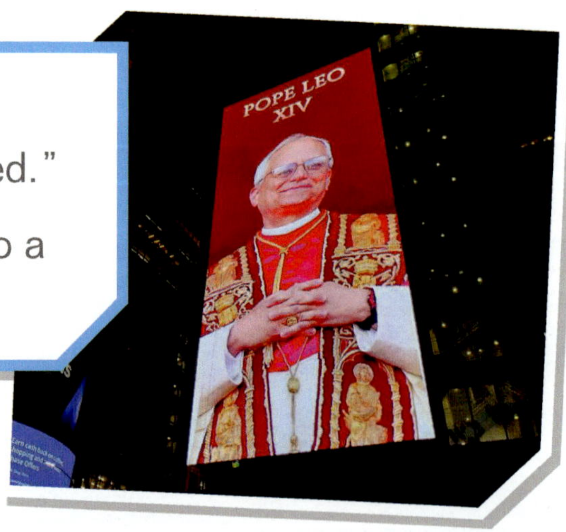

The Life of Pope Leo XIV

1955
Robert Francis Prevost was born on September 14 in Chicago, Illinois.

1969
Robert starts at St. Augustine Seminary High School.

1982
Robert is ordained an Augustinian priest in Rome.

1985
Robert goes to the Augustinian mission in Chulucanas, Peru.

1988
Robert joins the mission in Trujillo, Peru.

2001
Robert is elected the head of the Order of St. Augustine.

2015
Robert is named Bishop of Chiclayo in Peru.

2023
Robert moves to Vatican City and is named a cardinal.

2025
Robert is elected pope and takes the name Pope Leo XIV.

Many thought an American wouldn't be chosen as pope, but the other cardinals saw Robert Prevost as a leader who is an American *and* a Peruvian. He also speaks five languages and has years of experience as a leader.

WORLD LEADER

Pope Leo XIV's election was exciting for Catholics across the United States. They saw him as a fellow American—he's even a baseball fan who roots for the Chicago White Sox! Peruvians celebrated him as one of their own too. Others around the world respected his lifelong work for the poor.

Pope Leo's first speech was not as an American or a Peruvian but as a world leader. He encouraged the Catholic Church and all people to "build bridges" to seek peace. His words and deeds will continue to make a difference for years to come.

In His Words

"Help us, too, and help each other to build bridges, with **dialogue**, with meetings, uniting us all to be one people, always in peace."

— First speech as pope as reported by *Vatican News* from May 2025

Be Like Pope Leo XIV!

With the help of a trusted adult, organize an effort to help those in need, such as a food or clothing collection.

Share a toy or game with a friend.

Learn about the problems refugees face and how to help them.

Invite someone new into your friend group.

Get involved in community activities, such as cleanups and picnics.

If kids in your school or community speak a different language, learn words in that language so you can talk to them.

Learn about different countries around the world and the problems they face.

Build bridges by speaking kindly to people who are different from you and listening to them.

Pope Leo XIV is a teacher and leader to about 1.4 billion Catholics. You can be a teacher and leader in your own community!

GLOSSARY

bishop: An official in some Christian churches who is ranked higher than a priest and who oversees church matters in a certain area.

cardinal: A priest of very high rank in the Roman Catholic Church.

chimney: A hollow structure that allows smoke from a fire inside a building to escape outside.

degree: An official paper given to someone who has completed certain classes at a college or university.

dialogue: A conversation or discussion to resolve a problem.

diocese: An area under the leadership of a bishop.

diverse: Made up of people who are different from each other.

guerrilla: Having to do with irregular or secretive military methods.

immigrant: One who comes to a country to settle there.

mission: A building used by a religious group to spread its faith in the world. People called missionaries live and work there.

ordain: To officially make someone a religious leader in a ceremony.

priest: A man who performs religious ceremonies.

refugee: A person who leaves their home country to escape danger.

FOR MORE INFORMATION

WEBSITES

Pope
kids.britannica.com/kids/article/pope/353598#
Read more about what a pope's responsibilities are.

Pope Leo XIV Facts for Kids
kids.kiddle.co/Pope_Leo_XIV
Read more about this Catholic leader's life.

BOOKS

Bogner, Katherine. *We Have a Pope*. Steubenville, OH: Emmaus Road, 2024.

Slade, Suzanne. *Pope Francis*. New York, NY: Golden Books, 2024.

INDEX